PRIČA O BROJEVIMA

THE NUMBER STORY

SMALL BOOK ONE

ENGLISH - CROATIAN

*Numbers Teach Children
Their Number Names*

written and illustrated by

MISS ANNA

Early Reader Edition of *The Number Story 1*
Bronze Medal Winner, 2016 Wishing Shelf Book Award

Cover by | Lumpy Publishing
Layout by | Lumpy Publishing
Translated by Jovan Komlenac
Coloring by Jieeun Woo and Maria Mirabella

Library of Congress Control Number: 2018902040

Names: Miss Anna, author.
Title: Number story : numbers teach children their number names / Miss Anna.
Description: Portland, OR: Lumpy Publishing, 2018.
Identifiers: ISBN 978-1-945977-80-0| LCCN 2018902040
Summary: The pictures and rhymes present stories which introduce numbers 0-10.
Subjects: LCSH Numeration—English--Croatian--Pictorial works--Juvenile literature. | BISAC JUVENILE NONFICTION /
Languages: English--Croatian
Classification: LCC QA141.3 .M57 2018 | DDC 513—dc23

Publisher: Lumpy Publishing
Website: www.missannabooks.com
Email: missanna@missannabooks.com

Paperback: ISBN 978-1-945977-80-0
Printed in the U.S.A.   1 3 5 7 9 10 8 6 4 2

Želite li da naučite
nazive brojeva?

It is very easy and a lot of fun!

Veoma je lako i zabavno!

Say-along our little jingle

Otpjevajte sa nama našu malu priču!

starting from Number One!

Krenimo od broja jedan!

1

ONE looks like my one finger.

JEDAN

izgleda kao prst.

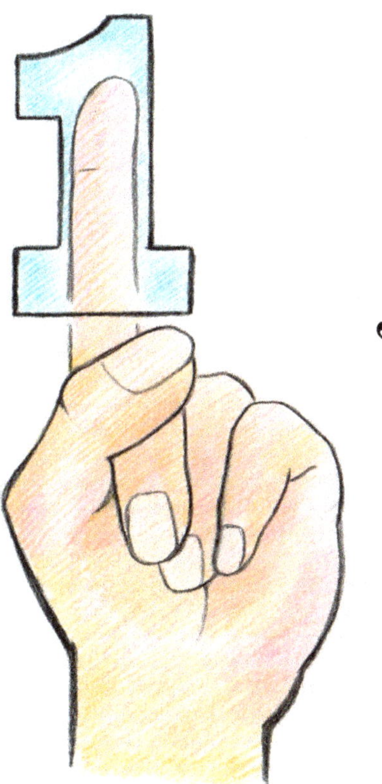

ONE!

JEDAN!

2

TWO   trails a tail.

DVA

ima rep.

A TAIL! REP!

3

THREE has bumps.

TRI

je kao brijeg.

BRIJEŽULJKAST JE!
Pogledajte ta zelena brda!

4

FOUR carries a sail.

ČETIRI ima jedro.

A SAIL!
BRODIĆ JEDRENJAK!

5

FIVE   is a racing track.

PET

je cesta za teretnjak.

VROOM
BRRRRM!
1

SIX curves like a snail.

ŠEST

se svija kao puž.

A SNAIL!   PUŽ!

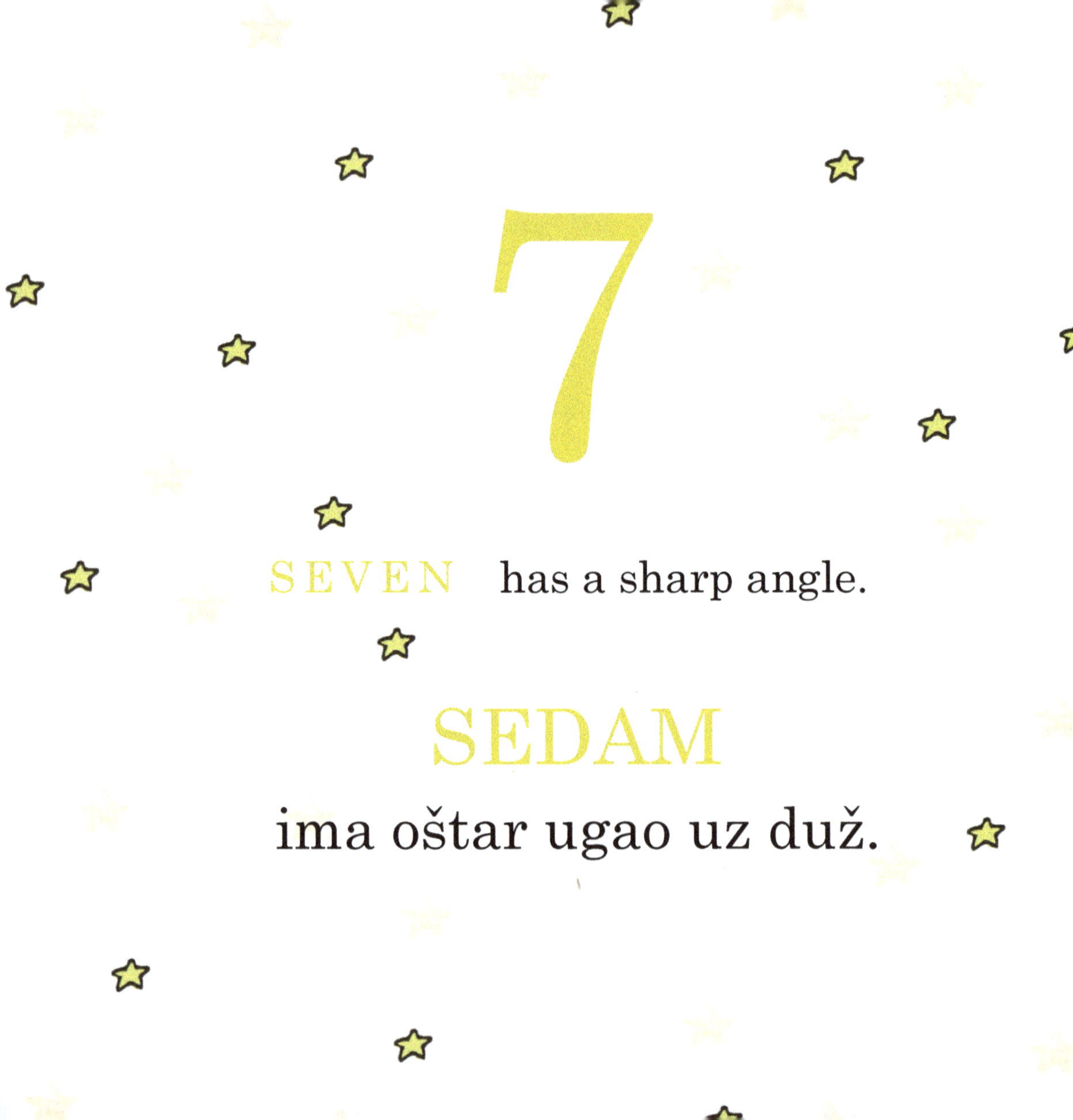
7

S E V E N has a sharp angle.

SEDAM

ima oštar ugao uz duž.

OUCH!
JAOJ!
BE CAREFUL! IT'S SHARP!
PAZI! OŠTRO JE!

8

E I G H T   is rollercoaster rails.

OSAM

je vlak u zabavnom parkiću.

JUPI!
YIPPEE!

NINE is a bubble on a stick.

DEVET

je balončić na štapiću.

A BUBBLE! BALONČIĆ!

TEN is an eye of a whale.

DESET

je jedno kitovo oko.

NAMIGUJE TI!
WINK!
HELLO! BOK!

And
I
0
ZERO   is an empty pail.

NULA
je prazna kofa koja
ima dno duboko.

IT'S EMPTY!
PRAZNO JE!

Thank you for playing with us today.

We had a lot of fun too!

Hvala što ste se igrali sa nama danas.

I nama je bilo mnogo zabavno!

We are your Number friends,
Zero to Ten,
Who will be here for you~
Mi smo tvoji prijatelji brojevi
Nula do Deset.
Uvjek ćemo biti tu za tebe.

Bye-bye now!
See you again soon.
Doviđenja!
Vidimo se uskoro!

The Numbers are *SINGING* too!

To sing-a-long, look for Miss Anna Number Story
at your favorite music store like iTUNES.

MP3

Numbers 0-10
IDENTIFYING
& COUNTING

Numbers 11-20
& Ordinals
first, second, third...

Numbers 0-100
& Place Values
ones, tens, hundreds...

About Clocks
& Telling Time
hours, minutes, seconds

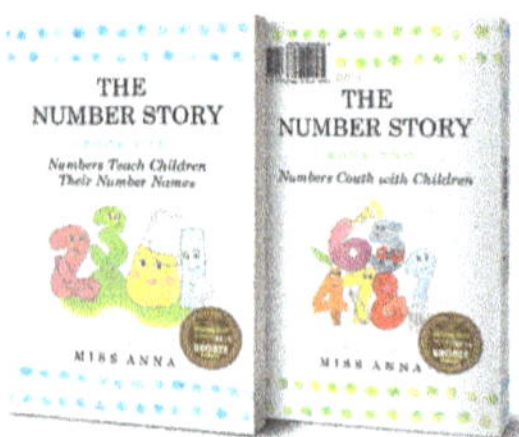

Number Story 1 & 2
isbn: 978-0-996216-48-7

Number Story 3 & 4
isbn: 978-1-945977-01-5

Number Story 5 & 6
isbn: 978-1-945977-06-0

Number Story 7 & 8
isbn: 978-1-949320-40-4

For more Miss Anna books to love,
visit us at

www.missannabooks.com

Numbers are working hard all over the world!
Come Travel the World with Us!

www.ingramcontent.com/pod-product-compliance
Lightning Source LLC
Chambersburg PA
CBHW040902070726
47599CB00035B/2278